Ravished

by Lydia Hack

My Inspirations

Dustin,

I love you and I know exactly why.

Nora & Beth,

You've turned my life upside down, the way it should be.

I will love you forever and that will never change.

I have perceiv'd that to be with those I like is enough,
To stop in company with the rest at evening is enough,
To be surrounded by beautiful, curious, breathing,
laughing flesh is enough,
To pass among them or touch any one, or rest my arm
ever so lightly round his or her neck for a moment, what
is this then?
I do not ask any more delight, I swim in it as in a sea.

-Walt Whitman, *I Sing the Body Electric*

rav ish

verb

1. seize and carry off (someone) by force.
2. fill (someone) with intense delight; enrapture.

- Oxford Dictionary

Contents

New Love

I.

Waterfall 'motions
lips done resisting distance
you ask to grab me

Slippery rock paths
your hands take a hold of me
hearts beat on joined lips

Harbor walks at night
touches, glances, deep eyes
raw intimations

"Walk me home," you say
press me up on misty steel
could take me right here

Knock. splitting kindling
"we will only sleep," I say
body fire rages

Clothes descend, hands find
you taste me from head to toe
pure fucking heaven

II.

Rain crashes on us
skiff lurches with fierce rhythms
begging us to mate

Occupied cabin
quietly I wake you
silent eruption

Salty tongues, warm flesh
you put in, I put out
contrasting hard and soft

Hard nipples, pinch tight
feel your lips on my pink lips
softly I'm quaking

Wait, it's the earth
Mother Earth agreeing
forces pushing us

Together, as one
magnetized bodies shifting
found new place of rest

III.

Seven times today
that pressure between my thighs
releases music

Your strong, worn, calloused
fingers shifting to reach my
chorus of pleasure

Two notes, one octave
two different vibrancies
love making cadence

Trees, waves, storms, light
your lyrics unite my mind
with life around

IV.

Your life within me:
two heart beats throbbing inside
two new lives forming

Taking Him for Granted

He adores me
but I want him
to adore me

He touches me
but I want him
to touch me

He fucks me
but I want him
to fuck me

He holds me
but I want him
to hold me

He loves me
but I want him
to love me

The One

I love watching you eat,
using your fork to conduct an orchestra
of tastes in your mouth,
slow, steady, rhythms of flavor

Headache

I've got a headache
a pressure in my ears like two hands pushing out
trying to break down their walls of confinement.

Old lovers
heartbroken losses
deep insecurities
thoughtless enemies
clawing at the plates of my head;
let them out!

What are they doing in there?
arguing, contemplating, fighting
their fists pounding on the inside of my skull;
get out!

Sex Dream

I wake up sweaty

The way he touched me,
his long dark hair loose and frizzy

He's a stranger,
a body I can't name,
but last night he made me tingle

Orgasm

Slow, tighten, hold
slow, tighten, hold
slow, tighten, hold

Tingling starts small
tighten, hold, slow
tingling expands
reaches up from my pelvis
past my stomach
to my heart
my neck
my mouth
my eyes

Whole body quivering,
crying

Letter to Abusive Friends

I will be kind to you because I am strong.

I will be kind to you in order to commemorate the moments your support was all I had.

I will be kind to myself by refusing your disdainful treatment of me.

I will surround myself with love that energizes, not depletes.

Shattered Words

I open my mouth,
words falling
like pellets of glass
on the untouched cement:
shattering, bouncing, slicing the bare soles
of each person unlucky enough to walk where I have
been.
I demand you to love me well, but this hate is all I have.
Rupturing my body, it leaves me open to the forces.
Lost in distrust and aged guilt, I trudge through the miry
land,
craving light and green,
but this fluid, this blood, pounds through my veins.
Will it stop my mind from intertwining with the
brilliance of touch?
With the sincerity of honest eyes?
With the determined voice?
Will it fight its way out?
Or keep this body cramped in contorted positions?

Now

Smoky breaths
dull my senses.
My postulant mind
listens, begs, embraces.

Sweet laughs.
Smooth tongues.
Heavy eyes.
I bare myself
to bear your weight.

What I want
you fight away;
you eat my heart,
consume my pride.

Your hand slips behind my soft curls.
Gently I look to you, asking —
no, begging.

You touch your mouth to my neck.
How can I want and hate you equally?
I move to you,

the hate hurls me forward.
It's not you I hate,
it's me.
It would remain
with your absence.

The coldness of your tongue
between my legs
is forbidden,
but it's mine, for this moment,
now.

The warmth of your lips
your forcing hands
I welcome them
tonight,
tomorrow,
now.

April Twenty-Third

Force me to my knees,
I pray.
I am worthless
without you.

I see the ugliness
in me
evident
in your eyes.
I will not stand,
nor will I sing
when I'd rather
run.

How can I
do anything else
when I carry this
weight?

The outcome screams
brokenness.
I get rid of it,
I am still left with me.

At least it
is
a
distraction.

Sitka

The pine trees are crying;
the sun that once illuminated their brilliance
has sunk into its cave.

Rhythmic dripping forms currents,
washing away the residue of passed time.

Rain reigns over this land.
It takes captives, creates life, feeds unhappiness.
It transforms stagnation into newness.

I become its captive
giving into the gloom,
letting the cold seep into me.

It chills, then tingles.
I will not fight it.

Dad

I hear his footsteps on the staircase; I immediately check
to see if I'm doing anything wrong.

Sitting up straight? Homework out on the desk? Bed
made? Music turned down? His presence, unannounced,
frightens me.

Even now. It is something I have grown to love about
him. His unpolished comments, his outrageous new
ideas,

his unrealistic passions, his simple mindedness. He's
genius, but no one seems to comprehend it.

He's abrasive and scary. But sometimes he's gentle,
understanding. He only sees ugliness in himself.

He sees all his incapacities. He lets depression rule his
heart. He's beautiful inside, but he's untouchable,
misunderstood.

He gets lost in new discoveries. He's always thinking,
analyzing, interpreting. He builds theories and
establishes uncommon beliefs.

He loves his wife and his God more than anything else.
He's proud of them. He's loyal. He lives for solitude,
silence, stars, sunrises.

His thoughts are his fuel. He understands the complex.

He hides in his office, afraid of his darkness hurting the
ones that he loves.
I wish he would break free and realize we want him next
to us.
We want him to be unguarded and open.
He doesn't think he has much to offer.
He does, but he doesn't know how to.
It breaks my heart to see his unhappiness.
I feel that unhappiness, too.

Ravished

The wind harasses me
pushing me over
leaving me confused and uncertain
about each step I take forward.
I fight it off with determination,
but my muscles are unable.
I need to find the confidence I elude to owning.
I think I know.
I think I have purpose,
but I feel like I am quickly approaching a cliff,
uncertain of when the wind will push me over
and slam me into the jagged rocks.
I am tired of feeling like I have something to prove.
I have nothing to prove.
I want to have the freedom just to be:
to be one. to be alone. to be together.
to be happy. to be angry. to protest.
to be the bitter one. to be deliberate. to be careful.
to be demanding. to be understanding.
to be loving. to be caring. to be selfless.
to be selfish. to be honest, open, stubborn.
I want to stand on that cliff and scream at the top of
my lungs.
I want to be heard.
I want to be shaken.
I want the wind to ravish my body.

Feeling Again

I rip my clothes off;

they're uncomfortable and constraining.

My eyes are tender from months of pent up emotions.

I'm feeling again.

You want me to trust you,

to confide in you,

but where the hell are you?

I cover my body with a dark shadow,

a cold blanket which brings no warmth.

No one's holding me tonight.

I wish life was simple again:

when crying meant someone would come hold me,

pick me up and try to make me smile.

I lay here,

curled in a ball

wondering why these tears are flowing now.

Feeling is good,

normal,

right.

My chest aches, but I need it.

I welcome it back,

but what do I do with it now that it's here again?

It can't shape or mold me.

It can only add to how I am, what I do, who I am.

I need this ache.

I need this pain, the tears.

I need this deep laughter, the joy.

I'm not ashamed of how I express myself.

It's what I feel.

I'm so tired of being on the defensive.

Take me.

If my silence is frightening,

if my emotions are overwhelming,

deal with it.

Control

I am craving peace of mind and focus.

Emotional distractors are constantly in my way.

I'm beginning to envy those who feel no pain because of their unattachment to love.

But feeling pain because of attachment to love is much more freeing.

Grinning, while hearing music in my ears, I realize I am where I am because of who I am.

Me. I did it.

I control my attachments, my emotional swings, my relationships, my passions, my knowledge.

I am in control.

Am I going to act like it or take the passive, easy way out?

Either way I am giving into a form of control.

My control should be a tool of empowerment, action.

My control should be contemplative, free, strong, full.

No second guessing, no not knowing.

A Letter to Friends

I am so thankful for your hearts.

I am full of support, love, happiness, anxiety, fear, and peace.

I want to grow from this relationship;

from our impressions on each other.

I feel imprints on my heart from the touches, whispers, screams, collisions we have had.

My heart is pounding, is bound, is expanding with desire to be more like you, to learn more, to experience more of you in my life.

My heart is always fighting something.

It's a darkness I can't shake.

It's a need to be ravished.

Ravished.

I want to see myself so clearly,

I don't question what's behind every decision, every step, every movement, every word, every emotion, every glance, every tear.

I am stymied by the psyche.

I am on a wheel: running, but staying still.

I am on a hike that has already been planned.

Is what I am doing evidence of evolutionary involvement?

This cycle. This fear that I really do not have a say in
how I respond, how I interact.

It's set.

My neurotransmitters are firing.

This life is a result of neurons, hormones, myelin
sheaths, cells dying and recreating.

This is beauty, and beauty is biology.

Beauty is my psyche responding to its life.

Beauty is nature.

Beauty is my species.

Beauty is my love.

Beauty is my pain.

Beauty is my breath.

Beauty is this poetry.

Beauty is being present.

Being here, now, with you, with rain,
with all the loves of my life.

No

With every movement
my form hardens
fighting back this
enticing
monster.
He suffocates me with his
poisonous lips.
His hands grip my face.
I am so close
to giving in.
One breath.
One touch.
Force me.
I won't say no.
Stay back.
Tie your hands and
do not make me fight.
My hands move over your
clenching body.
Your flesh is warm,
easy to peel away.
Exposed,
you are repulsive.
Your brilliant eyes
beg me for more.
I don't say no.

Bitter Lemons

No water here.
No mixture of substances.
This is my brain. concentrated.
Pour me out;
taste the bitterness on your tongue—
effortlessly sour.
Squint, cringe, stop the sweet.
Take it by the spoonful.
It's good for you:
medicinal,
concentrated.
My thoughts are strong;
emotions tense.
Concentrated.
Do not mix me.
My smile is not honey.
It's sour in here.
Bitter and sour.

Frankly

Shaking. *Sorry, but I just can't.*

You don't understand. My stomach aches. The cold
becomes insignificant in comparison to my nerves. My
lips are not chapped from the absence of chapstick, but
from my relentless tongue moving across them as I tell
you the truth behind these desiring eyes.

The excuses in my head compile rapidly. I'm too lost,
too unaffected by emotions to care about propriety.
I set myself free. But bind myself closer to you.

Lost in a Fantasy

I have these dreams
of what it would be like
to wake up next to you
in an alternate life.

You're different now;
I'm different.
I want to taste you,
to feel your hands discovering me;
your hands,
trembling lips,
quivering abs,
my soft tummy pressing against your
rock solid core:
moving,
making impressions.

Developed feelings;
years of push and pull,
mostly push.
I want to push my way into your bed.
I want to pull you down on top of me,

kiss your chest,
make love to you all night long.

What was I afraid of?

Tight white tank top
my nipples showing through.
I wanted you to rip it off,
You were in town then,
I should have let you rip it off.

What were we afraid of?
Falling?

Eerie

It is dark, but the sun is hinting its arrival with a subtle
glow of orange, visible above the trees.
I timidly step onto the street, cold silence wrapping
itself around my body like a blanket I don't want.
The click of my boots on the pavement is eerie.
I find myself carefully peeking over my shoulder in the
hopes that my imagination will be tamed;
it's running wild this morning.
I jump at the chirp of birds, the hum of a car, the
creaking of a front door opening.
Normally silence comforts me, but this morning I crave
sound.
I fumble for my iPod, hoping it will set me free in a
world of melodies.
Battery almost dead, it warns me.
My fingers, too cold to emerge from my warm felt-lined
pockets, find 'play.'
The three second wait before a song starts is abnormally
painful:
Haydn's cello concerto in C begins.
Instantaneous peace spreads through me.
My surroundings are reborn, now overcome by beauty.

I notice the freshness of the air, the fabulous colors of the sun.

My solitude in this sleeping neighborhood is welcomed.

Successfully saved from my wandering thoughts—I'm anew.

Motherhood

I used to write,
but my thoughts wander
through the words I need
to place on this paper—
no direction, no emotion;
torn from my fingertips too soon.

The delicate process of structuring
sentences, words, feelings
is more like taking handfuls
of made up words
and throwing them
towards the boring lines of my notebook.

I'm too tired to make sense,
to think deep,
to focus.
Doesn't matter.
Write. Keep writing.
Keep writing and eventually the words
meld together like dough,
reaching out their scraggly arms
to hold onto themselves.

Writing is how I hold onto myself.
Where have I been? Who is this?

Penning words onto lonely paper
is my arms grasping at my body
wrapping it up in understanding,
in me.

Daughter

Tight little curls separated by the wind
Flowers tickling her nose
Her chicken in her arms
Her mind rising towards the sun

Full of perseverance
that tires her mama
Emotions shaping her face into wild expressions:
her mouth wide with cries,
all her teeth showing,
tongue reaching for comfort from the roof of her
mouth,
her eyes destitute for understanding.

She wants to be held,
to breathe in the scent of her mama—
the scent of comfort.

She reaches for her.
Her mama's arms envelop her little body.
Returning to mama's chest
Heartbeats matching in time:
stabilizing,
renewing.

Eleanor

Curly wings, wispy
yellow and fragile short strands
flying loose from the wind

Desert sand between
eyelashes and fingernails
mixing dirt with mud

Little girl on quests:
learning, fighting, being young
full of fierce powers

Elisabeth

Tearing roots from ground
feet covered in small pokies
scooping piles of dirt

Hopeful little eyes
effortlessly determined
like plants finding rain

Climbing up fences
purple flowers in her hands
discovering life

Finding dead insects
breathing magic into them
nurturing new life

Anxiety Attack

Every night
my head rotates
on its axis:
constant rotation,
meteors landing.
craters forming,
lives ending,
breaths stopping,
panic ensuing,
eyes diving into corners,
heart rapid firing,
machine gun bursts,
blood turning black—
black and dark.
When will this end?
This nightmare;
this anxiety

Attachment Theory

Your attachment theory is flawed.

What are you

but this bag of drooping flesh

following the gravitational forces of admiration?

Stretching, folding, careening forward.

Develop this habit. Develop that hobby.

Will they approve of you?

Will you follow them

blindly down the road of alcoholism,

of risky sexual behaviors,

of wild beliefs, of mad love?

Are you desperate for acceptance?

Are you desperate to be discovered?

Devoured?

Fawned over?

Assault

He had tattoos all over his arms:

robotic fetuses,

sickening, creepy, and evil.

I don't remember his name.

I've erased it from my brain.

He was dark,

Middle Eastern.

He smelled like coffee and weed.

He owned a café

in a hot stuffy mall.

He was a connection—

a friend of my cousins—

someone to show me around a foreign city.

He bought me dinner,

took me to a club,

handed me shots of arak.

He showed no interest;

I showed even less.

It wasn't until later that I realized

he had not drank anything.

He drove me back to his apartment.

The world was spinning around me.

I think he kissed me.

He told me I could sleep on his bed
and that he'd take the guest room.

I passed out in his bed, fully clothed.

I woke up to my dress pushed up,
my panties missing,
his face between my legs.

I was in a foggy daze.

I tried to push his face way.
He pulled his pants down.
He pinned my arms down and put his penis in my face.
"It's my turn," he said.
I turned my head to the side and tried to push him off
harder.
He grabbed my face and turned it to his dick.
I shook my head vehemently.
He grabbed my face again,
saying louder,
"It's my turn!"

I managed to kick him off.
I ran into the guest bedroom and locked the door.
I barricaded myself in there.
Afraid.
Ashamed.
Confused.

I hid in that room until he left for work
the next morning.
He knocked on my door.
I didn't answer. I waited
and waited
and waited.
He finally left.
I waited longer.

I gathered my things,
left his keys in the electrical box,
got on the 444.
I stared out the window,
watching the flora change from green to brown;
the sun heavy with heat
my eyes red, unable to blink.

The Battle

There was a type of peace that shook me with each
raindrop that hit my dry skin.
I felt the filth washing away:
the depression, the ugly darkness covering my heart was
being eaten by rain.
I am so tired of fighting myself:
constantly on guard, hoping the next thrust of my
sword doesn't murder my soul.
I have been careless with the weapon.
Every fight hurts me more.
The pain goes a little deeper.
I seem to think that each new wound will help me feel
something more.
How could I be so stupid? Wounds don't make you feel
more alive; they kill you.
They leave you convulsing on the ground, writhing in
your own miserable pity, drawing attention to your
carelessness.
But I don't know how to function without pain and fear:
always on the defensive, always ashamed of myself.
I am reaching for something.
Someone.
I'm unsatisfied.

I have nothing to offer anyone,

except my hollow body,

and even that I'm not proud of.

Yes, men like to look at me.

They like to fuck me,

but what if all the dirt that I hide inside was exposed?

Everyone would run.

I pretend to be happy,

to have it together,

but really, I'm screaming inside—

screaming for something safe.

I can't trust God,

or maybe I just don't know how because there's not a

single man in my life I trust.

I don't know how to relate to a father.

I was taught to be weak around men.

I come to God when I'm weak.

I run to men when I'm weak.

And if I'm not weak around men I fuck up until I am;

until they can somehow fix it,

to put me back in that comfortable place of not being

good enough.

I'm so tired of myself.

I'm so tired of destroying myself.

Lover

Worn truth in your eyes
I stare into them, thankful,
don't need words to see.

Passionate and strong:
our bodies envelop love—
pure, alive, and one.

Am I Such a Good Wife

Am I such a good wife
that I crave outside attention?
that I fantasize over other men?
men I don't know,
men I do know,
men I have known?

Am I such a good wife
that I cry when I should be smiling?
scold when I should be approaching?
retreat when I should be charging?

Am I such a good wife
that I give you everything you want,
everything you need,
just for your approval?

Am I such a good wife?
You better fucking believe it.

Haifa

Find me here,
harmonica wistfully soothing inharmonious chords,
trying to replicate the complexities of previously crafted
melodies.
Imperfection is welcomed, needed, sought.
Bring imperfection to my side; wrap it around my course
heart,
my unsmooth skin.

I'm alone here,
solitude ravishing this body.
It fights, seduces, intoxicates.
It folds me away from sought purpose,
beats me until my confidence is bled out.
Teetering on faux passion, eliciting glances, desiring eyes
—

my heart craves only one;
my body craves many.

Here, my tongue trembles,
will you speak?
Here, my eyes pierce,
will you stay?

Affair

His wedding ring caught her eye.

Not a deterrent—

it brought comfort.

The brilliance of its shine was luring her to him.

His eyes see me. He somehow understands my loneliness.

He reached for the Tanqueray.

It splashed carelessly on the counter as it hit

the overflowing ice in her glass.

She smiled comfortably.

His hands moved methodically as he sliced a lime.

She wondered if his hands would be as confident on her

skin.

She was lost in every movement he made,

captivated.

She lifted the glass to her lips, hoping the familiar taste

would satisfy.

He watched her mouth carefully, imagining the softness

behind it.

Her lips were tender.

The way they moved over her teeth made his hands

shake.

Her long curls fell invitingly on her bare collar bone.

His gaze rested on her neck.

She could feel the heat of his desire.

The intensity was extreme.

She ached for the extreme.

So did he.

But this extreme was fatal.

Accepting it killed what she stood for.

It suffocated her heart.

My Firefighter

Where has the fire gone?
It's there, dig a lil deeper.
But are you sure, babe?

I don't feel it now.
I'm here, touching you, my love.
But I can't feel it.

Where has the fire gone?
It's here, in your open palm.
But I can't see it.

Your eyes used to burn.
They still do. They burn for you.
But are you sure, babe?

Man of Stature

What am I to do with you,
you man of stature?
You're a king among men—
a fighter.
You're tender,
loyal,
strong-willed,
fierce.
You rock my world
sexually.
You complete me.
I've never been so satisfied.
I've never lost my heat for you,
but the spark,
the glances,
the butterflies—
they've gone.

In the beginning,
our touches electrified;
they shocked;
they brought this tsunami
of animalistic passion.
My body physically longed for you

when we were apart.
I could feel the weights forcing us back
together.

I nit-pick.
I pry.
I give-in.
I'm tired.

I'm here,
but I'm missing.

I'm with you,
but I'm lost.

Have I wrapped my
identity up in this
so much
I can't think?

Where do we go?

You love me madly, you say,
but I don't feel it.
I don't feel it.
I don't fucking feel it.
Why can't you love
like you used to?

Once we get to this place,
how do we get the fire back?
What match in this box of matches
is the right one?

Strike it.
Light it.
Ignite my soul.

We were meant
from the beginning
to be together.

Our flames
could burn down
forests.

I'm here,
prodding the glowing coals.
Smoke gets in my eyes—
stinging, burning.

All we need
is a little kindling.
The flames will come back.

A little kindling;
a little air.

My Sweet Darlings

I love holding your hand,
watching your eyes tire,
fingers relaxing into my palm.
I love singing to you,
laying down with you,
holding you as you drift off to sleep.

I'm your momma,
etching every flicker of your soul
into mine.

You beautiful creatures of mine—
sleeping quietly,
awakening me for every fright,
for every nightmare,
for every ache.

I will protect you.
I'll sing you back to sleep.

I'll hold you close
when your emotions are too strong for your tiny bodies.
I'll hold you close

when your tears aren't taking away the pain.

I'll hold you close

when your laughter is covering up fear.

I'll hold you close

when your happiness reaches the tips of your toes.

I'll hold you close

when your eyes sparkle with pride.

I'll hold you close

when you tell me your dreams.

I'll hold you close

when you go the wrong way.

I'll hold you close.

I'll whisper into your ear:

I will love you forever
and that will never change.

Rhythms

We move together,
dancing to slow melodies
of peace and momentous rhythms.

Let it Go

Adjust.
Go with the flow.
Breathe.
Be present in the moment.

Let old and past prejudices go.
Focus on the sun;
the way champagne bubbles on your tongue,
wakening the nerves,
waiting for a new taste;
a laugh;
breathing in fresh air,
breathing in slowly,
deliberately.

You cause your own suffering
and your own freedom.

Let it go.
All the bitterness—
let it go.

Tranquility

Breathing in the mists from the pouring rain —
I lay beside you.
Your hand forms around the gentle curve of my hips,
quaking my nerves,
gliding quietly across my stomach.
It finds its home on my chest.
I am overcome.
It vibrates through me,
a never-ending wave.
Your touch brings peace
and ignites passion.

Mother. My Mother

She taught me love
and how to smile.

She taught me strength
and how to laugh while I'm crying.

She taught me beauty
and how to find it in hopeless moments.

She taught me patience
and how to accept mistreatment.

She taught me forgiveness
and how to hold a grudge.

She taught me perseverance
and how to be free.

She taught me respect
and how to stand proud.

She taught me melodies
and how to cook a meal.

She taught me compassion
and how to be a mother.

Pregnancy

I'm sitting down,
abdomen resting on my lap,
listening to the gentle movement of the water
lapping up around weather-formed rocks.
The sun is glistening and sharing its warmth with me.
The air is still, occasionally whispering through the
shrubs and pines
about the plants that are on their way to being reborn,
syncing the evolvement of seasons with the growth of
my babies.
I will do all it takes to care for them,
to believe in them,
to nourish their hearts.

Wounds

I don't want to go there—

that deep dark gaping wound.

I'll cover it up;

pretend it doesn't hurt me.

It doesn't hurt me.

Really.

It's numbed me.

I'm tired;

tired of feeling numb,

of feeling barely anything when you touch me.

What did I do?

Why did I let her weasel her way into our relationship?

Into our passion?

A wedge

hammered in between my body and yours;

its splinters hurt me.

Why did I allow it?

I thought we were whole,

but we weren't.

I thought we were untouchable,

but we weren't.

I thought we could recover,

but we haven't.

It hurts me.
I'm telling you it hurts me,
but I know it doesn't hurt you,
not one tiny bit.
What gave you pride
gave me demise.

Probably Painful

What must it be like
to be the favorite—
the one who does no wrong?

Why Do You Stay?

Sometimes I wonder how
you kept it to yourself
and didn't stop it.
Have you never heard
of ultimatums?
of standing up to the abuse?
of telling him to stop?
of getting the fuck out?
of screaming back?
of taking your kids and leaving?

Would I do the same?

Giving Birth

Giving birth
to twin daughters
five minutes apart:
a bond so strong,
my body could barely handle it.
Their tiny bodies
ripped me open.
Their unbreakable spirits
threw me against the wall.
They showed me the bounds of love,
the fierceness of motherhood,
the tenderness of life.
Their souls linked together
to mine:
inseparable spirits
fighting,
breathing,
growing.

Raging Ocean

His emotions are like
a raging, untamed ocean:
you sit in a dinky canoe
and let the waves crash over you.
You explain it away:
it's a good ocean,
a beautiful ocean;
it offers life to so many.
You sit there, powerless,
and let the ocean rage.
You care more for the ocean than your soul.
The ocean will kill you.
Don't let it kill your soul.
Become the moon
and move the tides
from afar.

Mean

I wasn't being mean to you.
Yes you were.
I didn't say that.
Yes you did.
I didn't mean it.
Yes you did.

Hold Your Children

When your child cries,
open your arms.
Tell her it's okay to feel,
to hurt,
to ache,
in the parts of her body
she didn't know
could hurt.

Confronting the Past

I stood in my living room
telling you you're not a safe man

Do you remember the hurt you caused?

the clenching teeth
the choking
the punching of holes in the wall
the throwing of sharp objects towards my face
the hate fuming from your eyes

You once told me my path led to death and destruction.

If this life of mine is what death and destruction looks
like, hallelujah.

Stop Preaching

Stop preaching your lies
about sex and sin.
You are the sinner;
I am the saved.
You know nothing
except pride and disillusionment.

You think God cares about your wallet,
your lost keys.
No prayer is too small
to bring to God,
you say.

How can He hear the cries
of girls being raped,
boys being abused,
children starving,
mothers holding their lifeless babes
if you are filling the space
with your menial prayers?

Stop asking for senseless answers
to foolish prayers.
Treat God with respect;
don't waste His time.

Divine Intervention

If you think something, ignore it.
if you feel something, ignore it.
if something hurts you, ignore it.

Don't trust your feelings.
Your feelings are wrong.
They cannot guide you.

Your feelings are sinful.
Your emotions lead you astray.
Your brain should control your heart.

No, wait—
the white man behind the pulpit
knows your feelings.
They are sinful.
He will control your heart.

Your humanity is sinful.
Your lust is sinful.
Your spaghetti straps are sinful.
Your hand holding is sinful.

Your drinking is sinful.

Your smoking is sinful.
Your late-night friendships are sinful.

If you are alone
with a man
in a room
you are doomed to whoredom.

He won't be able to control himself
and you should have known better.
Your spaghetti straps told him
you are a whore.

Your lipstick told him
you are a whore.
He knows more than you
because you don't know your feelings;
you were taught not to trust them.

The white man behind the pulpit
can remove the spaghetti straps
and convince you

white evangelical authority
equals
divine intervention.

Past Love

I remember sitting with you:
our backs pressed up against
the cold cement wall;
the tiny wood stove
keeping our intertwined toes
warm.

Our relationship was heavy.
It carried a weight
that sent you reeling
into philosophical debates
with your soul.

I remember watching you sulk
in the corner,
wondering why my steadfastness
and my reluctance was
somehow yours to own.

I remember wondering
if all men act like victims
because every man I have known
pouts like a baby.

My Body

My long legs
My soft lips
I love them

My bright eyes
My determined tongue
I love them

I turn and stare at myself in the mirror.
Who is this woman
with the golden hair,
the pale glow?

I tilt my head back
and laugh
full throttle—
overbite teeth jutting out
over my sunken chin
I love them

This body of mine
withstood childbirth:
the creation of two lives

I stare at the curves of my thighs,
the constellations of stretch marks,
the loosened skin on my breasts
I stare and stare and stare
I love them

This body of mine
withstood depression,
assault, abuse, self-loathing

This body of mine
has shared love,
has been loved,
has given love

This body of mine
stands with grace,
moves with pride,
rises with might
I love it

Not Yours to Take

"Let me have it."

"But it's not yours!"

"Pretend it is!"

First Night Away From Them

I am panicking and my heart is beating fast.
I can't sleep.
My mind is racing.
I want my man's arms.
I miss my babies.
Calm me down
one word at a time.

One,

two,

three,

four,

five,

six,

seven,

eight,

nine,

ten,

eleven.

Greatest Hike of My Life

I watch your smile
and I realize
this is the greatest hike of my life,
even if I'm tired
and need to rest;
even if I need to pull out my map
and follow the meandering lines
through crevices and escarpments,
through peaks and valleys.

Boulders fall through my path,
making me want to turn around
to find an alternate way,
but I have to keep fighting
because this hike has the most
spectacular destination.

I will falter,
I will wail,
I will shout,

but I'm mesmerized
by the formations of Earth
under my tired toes.
I will stay the course
expectantly,
purposefully,
eagerly.

I Went to the Mountains

I went to the mountains
to climb and climb,
to feel my muscles tighten,
to feel them stretch.

Sometimes the only way to grow
is to climb a mountain.

You reach the summit,
wind howling, pushing you back.
You stand your ground.

You spread your arms wide,
leaning into the wind,
feeling your cheeks tighten.

You listen to the stories it tells.
It tells you its secrets—
the hills it has demolished,
the power it generates,
the earth it created,
the terrain it eroded.

You listen deeper.
It tells you to keep moving,
to stand proud,
but keep moving.

The only way to grow
is to keep moving.

The Rain Has Arrived

The rain has arrived.
It clears the air
of pollen and dust,
of particles that confuse your nose,
and stifle your throat.

It adds moisture to your crinkly hair.
Your lungs can breathe deeply,
easily,
freely.
They fill and deflate,
fill and deflate.

The rain has arrived,
has washed away
the pollution and the sludge,
the grime surrounding your heart,
building up in your veins.

The rain has arrived.
The humidity tickles your arms,
swells your fingers,
relaxes your muscles,
stretches your heart.

Enchantress

Your words bite me
with clenched teeth,
biting down hard.
A crocodile fighting its prey:
the sweet taste of pain
oozing from its face
sustains your life—
a reason to exist.

You are the worst person I know:
a pathetic human,
ruptured and broken,
rotting and putrid.

You dig your claws into
every beautiful soul you meet
and shred them to oblivion.

I've never met anyone as angry as you.
You guise it well,
but your demons can't hide for long.
They creep through your pores,
masquerading themselves
as an enchantress—
seductive and beguiling.

Chicago Winter Love

We partied on trains,
danced on rooftops,
our Arnold Palmers in tow.
My blue socks stretched above my knees.
It was cold outside.
My thrift store boots were tearing open,
the Chicago winter slush creeping in.

I rested my hand on your leg,
so happy to be together.

We were in love:
young,
vibrant,
adoring.

I laid down next to you—
your mattress
inches from the floor,
staring into your blue eyes,
your curly hair tangling
around my long fingers.
We laughed so much,

just laid there laughing,
touching,
kissing.

We danced to ridiculous music,
hands floating in the air,
bobbing heads,
drinking whiskey sours.

grand gestures
and deep dish pizza

We found love in that city
for a moment in time
and it was lovely.

The Formation of Words

Flecks of gold in my eyes
floating,
muddy mountain
sloping,
imagery
colors
shapes
emotions
blues and greens
oranges and fire
floods and canyons
strength and weakness.

I write to build the emotions
into a formation I can understand:
circles and lines
block by block
keep building
layer after layer.

When the words
travel from my brain
through my heart

and then down

down

down

to my fingers

strokes of my pen,

gliding over

slivers of trees

connecting me back to the earth,

the ground I'm born from

gifting me the words,

shapes and colors.

I need to care for my breathing body

that rises with the plants

and exalts the blue—

the water and sky—

with praise and healing.

Crows flaunting their feathers,

dark and endearing,

notice their courage,

their stamina,

squawking through

the passing time.

words

shapes

colors

emotions

Blend them together

place them awkwardly

on the page—

move, shift, combine.

Everything isn't beautiful at first.

Words need space to grow,

to breathe,

to reseed themselves.

They blossom slowly;

healing souls,

easing emotions,

waking peace.

Share Your Truth

If my words,
if my truth,
if my pain
that you caused
hurts you back—
now that I have power of my own,
you deserve it.

I don't know what pain you are harboring
inside
that is causing you to lash out,
but don't pout because I am sending my truth
into the vastness.

I don't want to lash out
at the ones I love
because of repressed emotions.

I am done bending my truth
to fit inside yours
when you don't even know what your truth is.

Free your truth—

send it out into the darkness
and watch as your chest
turns from hollow to solid.

This is my truth.
It is not yours.
I will not bend it,
mold it,
or meld it
into something other than what it is
to protect your precious feelings.

For all I know
your feelings will be hurt for the rest of time.

The Patriarchy

didactic words.
counterfeit morals.
patronizing beast.
despotic power.

angry stances.
aggressive tone.
righteous life.
coy wives.

temper tantrums.
forgotten children.
governed uteruses.
darkened eyes.

pity parties.
written contracts.
slammed doors.
broken eggshells.

Hidden Powers

My power is there—
deep inside.
I don't flaunt it
like you do.
I don't need to,
for I know how
powerful I am.

Partners

The first time
I pulled back from you;
the first time
I tightened up
on the reins,
you respected me more.

The first time
I called you out,
disagreed with you,
fought with you,
you listened intently;
you tried to see my point of view.

Not once did my opinions
hurt your feelings.

Not once did my truths
become a weapon
for you to control me with.

Not once have you
tried to control

my emotions,
my actions,
my thoughts.

I felt free the moment
I partnered
my life
with yours.

What Does a Tantrum Look Like?

This is a grown man's tantrum:

holes in walls

broken door frames

shattered chairs

combative tones

fiery eyes

This is a child's tantrum:

red face

crying

yelling

rolled up in a ball

legs squirming

eyes desperate for love

If you lovingly help a child
work through her tantrums,

she will not punch holes in walls

and

she will learn

to walk away from someone

who does.

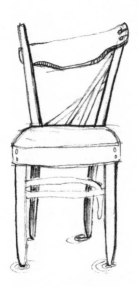

Victim

Stop playing the victim.
You are not a victim.
And if you were:
write it down,
express it,
get it out,
heal.

Soul Mate

How often do you
find a soul mate
that wraps her heart
around yours
and holds you up
when you are falling?

How often do you
find a soul mate
who selflessly
loves your children
simply because
they are
extensions of you?

How often do you
find a soul mate
who has the same
twinkle of pride
in her eyes
when your life
brings celebrations?

How often do you
find a soul mate
who weeps with you
when you are
alone and afraid?

How often do you
find a soul mate
who laughs with you
when laughing is the
only thing left to do?

To My Readers

Life sends you moments that define you.
Life also sends you people who define you.

Don't let the people define you.
Define yourself
in every moment,
in the changes,
shifts.
New identities form.
Hold onto all of them.
They are the reason you are here.

You can be many:
lover
maker
mover
mother
fighter
hater
ally.

You can be one.
You can be all
you.

About the Author

Lydia Hack has a BS in Human Ecology from The Ohio State University and is currently pursuing a MA in Marriage and Family Therapy. She has always been in awe of the beauties, intricacies, and patterns of relationships and how they impact our mental health and emotions. Over the years Lydia has turned to poetry in order to express these emotions. She has used the formation of words as a means to heal, as a way to stabilize, and as an outlet for speaking her truth. Lydia is a stay at home mother of twins, a baker of bread, and has lived all over the U.S. She hopes to one day move back to Sitka, Alaska where most of her story took shape.

CPSIA information can be obtained
at www.ICGtesting.com
Printed in the USA
LVHW111801080120
642936LV00009B/1250/P

9 780578 592312